Glass

Kate Walker

A+

Smart Apple Media

This edition first published in 2005 in the United States of America by Smart Apple Media.

Smart Apple Media
1980 Lookout Drive
North Mankato
Minnesota 56003

Library of Congress Cataloging-in-Publication Data

Walker, Kate.
  Glass / by Kate Walker.
  p. cm. — (Recycle, reduce, reuse, rethink)
  Includes index.
  ISBN 1-58340-557-7 (alk. paper)
  1.Glass—Juvenile literature. I. Title. II. Series.

  TP857.3.W33 2004
  666'.14—dc22   2003070409

First Edition
9 8 7 6 5 4 3 2 1

First published in 2004 by
MACMILLAN EDUCATION AUSTRALIA PTY LTD
627 Chapel Street, South Yarra, Australia,   3141

Associated companies and representatives throughout the world.

Copyright © Kate Walker 2004

Edited by Helena Newton
Text and cover design by Cristina Neri, Canary Graphic Design
Technical illustrations and cartoons by Vaughan Duck
Photo research by Legend Images

Printed in China

Acknowledgements

The author and the publisher are grateful to the following for permission to reproduce copyright material:

Cover photograph: glass production line, courtesy of Digital Vision.

Artville, p. 5 (jars, salt & pepper); Chris Jenkins, Aurora Glass Foundry, p. 24 (bottom); D. Parer & E. Parer-Cook/Auscape International, p. 16; Coo-ee Picture Library, p. 22; Delft Integraal, © Amdade Rieffe with permission, p. 17; Gina Payne & Maxine Childs, GardenMax, p. 27 (top); Getty News, p. 14; Great Southern Stock, pp. 9, 12, 18; Ibiza Eco Logic, p. 25 (both); MEA Photo, p. 5 (casserole dish); Oxford Scientific Films Limited, p. 15; © Jeremy Horner/Panos Pictures, p. 11; Photodisc, pp. 5 (bottle), 8, 29 & design features; Richard Lloyd, Recovered Materials Foundation, p. 26; J. Barrett, Recycled Bottle Glass Centre Ltd, p. 27 (bottom); Reuters, p. 20; Robert Long Consultancy Ltd UK, p. 21 (both); The Derby Telegraph, p. 24 (top); The G.R. "Dick" Roberts Photo Library, p. 10; VISY Recycling, pp. 19, 23.

Contents

Let's start recycling now!

When a word is printed in **bold**, you can look up its meaning in the glossary on page 31.

Recycling

Recycling means using products and materials again to make new products instead of throwing them away.

Why recycle?

Developed countries have become known as "throw-away societies" because they use and throw away so many products, often after just one use! Single-use products include drink cans, glass jars, sheets of paper, and plastic bags. Today, there are approximately six billion people in the world. By the year 2050, there could be as many as nine billion people. The world's population is growing fast, and people are using a lot more products and materials than they did in the past.

Instead of throwing products away, we can recycle them. When we recycle:

- ♻ we use fewer of the Earth's **natural resources**
- ♻ manufacturing is "greener" because recycling creates less **pollution** than using **raw materials**
- ♻ we reduce waste, which is better for the environment.

Governments, industries, communities, and individuals all around the world are finding different ways to solve the problems of how to conserve resources, reduce manufacturing pollution and waste, and protect the environment. If the Earth is to support nine billion people in the future, it is important that we all start recycling now!

As well as recycling, we can:

- ♻ reduce the number of products and materials we use
- ♻ reuse products and materials
- ♻ rethink the way we use products and materials.

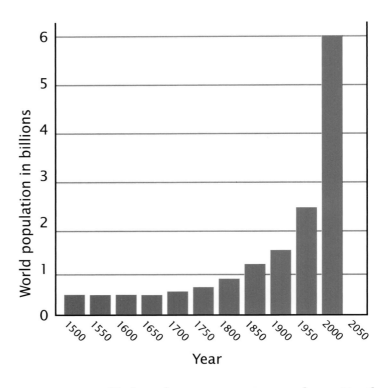

Today, there are more people on Earth using more products and materials than in the past, and the population is still growing.

What is glass?

Glass is sand that has melted and turned into a solid, shiny mass.

The history of glass

In nature, glass is made when lightning strikes desert sand and melts it. It is also made when red hot lava containing silica, the main mineral in sand, flows from volcanoes and cools. In about 5000 B.C., Phoenician sailors made glass by accident. They built a fireplace on a beach using stones made of a substance called soda. The heat of the fire melted some of the soda and the soda lowered the melting point of the sand. Next morning, the surprised sailors found lumps of glass in the ashes of their fireplace.

By 1500 B.C., the ancient Egyptians had learned how to make glass vessels to hold oil and wine. The art of glass making quickly spread from Egypt right around the world.

Glass products today

Today, glass is used for:

- ↻ food jars and drink bottles
- ↻ windows
- ↻ lightbulbs
- ↻ cookware and tableware
- ↻ **glazing** for pottery cups and bowls
- ↻ **fiberglass**.

We use many of these glass products every day.

How glass is

Some glass is sent to **landfills** and some is recycled. The average household in a developed country throws away 134 pounds (61 kg) of glass each year.

The glass that is recycled goes through many processes.

1

People put their used glass bottles and jars out for curbside collection.

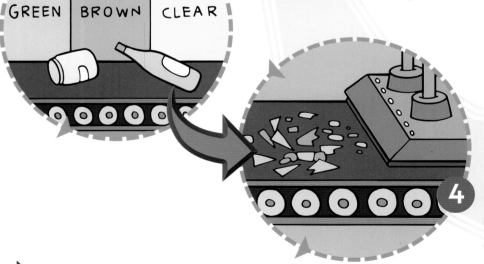

2 **The glass is collected by a truck and taken to the recycling center.**

At the recycling center, jars and bottles are sorted into pure streams of clear, green, and brown colored glass. Green and brown glass are not mixed because together they would make an unattractive, muddy brown color.

3

GREEN   BROWN   CLEAR

4 **Each pure stream of colored glass is crushed into small pieces, called cullet, for reprocessing.**

recycled

7 Molten glass is drawn from the furnace and made into new glass products.

8 New products made from recycled glass are bought by consumers.

6 At the glass factory, the cullet is added to **molten glass** in a glass **furnace**.

FURNACE

134 pounds (61 kg) of glass = 172 empty half-liter glass bottles

5 The cullet is washed to get rid of glue and food. Metal and plastic bottle caps are removed before the cullet is sent to the glass factory.

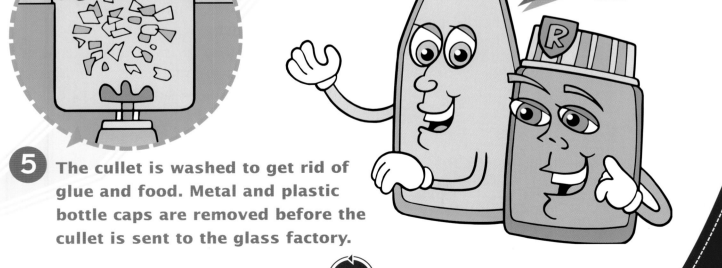

Recycled glass

Used glass products can be recycled into the same products again, or they can be made into very different products. The end products made from recycled glass depend on whether the glass is recycled in a closed or an open loop.

Closed-loop recycling

Closed-loop recycling happens when used materials are remade into new products again and again. The materials go round in a non-stop loop and are never wasted.

A closed-loop cycle

Closed-loop glass products

Some used glass products that can be recycled in a closed loop are:

🔄 *glass jars and bottles of the same color* These are made into new glass jars and bottles, which are clear, green, or brown in color.

🔄 *glass of mixed colors* This is ground into fine particles and added to **asphalt** on playground and road surfaces. Asphalt surfacing is 100 percent recyclable. It can be ripped up, crushed, and reheated to make new surfacing.

🔄 *ground glass* This is used in sandblasting machines. Sandblasters shoot grains of sand or recycled glass at metal and brick surfaces to clean off rust and old paint. The grains are saved and used again and again.

Asphalt, used for road surfaces, contains recycled glass.

products

Open-loop recycling

Open-loop recycling happens when used materials are made into products that cannot be recycled again. The materials are reused only once and then thrown away. Many people believe this is not recycling at all because the materials are wasted.

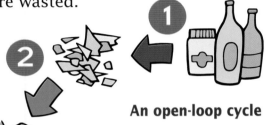

An open-loop cycle

Open-loop glass products

Some used glass products and materials that are recycled in an open loop are:

🔄 *mixed glass*   This is made into fiberglass. Fiberglass is made when glass is spun into fine threads, woven into mats, and coated with melted plastic. Fiberglass is used to make surfboards, roofing sheets, boat hulls, and much more. The glass in fiberglass can never be separated from the plastic, so it cannot be recycled again.

🔄 *fine grains of crushed glass*   These are glued onto heavy paper to make sandpaper. The grain side of the paper is rubbed against rough surfaces to make them smooth. The grains fall off and are lost.

🔄 *fine beads of ground glass*   These are added to roadmarking paint. The tiny beads reflect car headlights and make the lines light up at night. The paint wears away and the glass beads are lost.

🔄 *ground glass of mixed colors*   This is used to cover garbage in landfill sites.

Why recycle

When we recycle used glass products to make new glass products:

- ↻ we use fewer of the Earth's natural resources
- ↻ manufacturing is "greener" because recycling creates less pollution than using raw materials
- ↻ we reduce waste, which is better for the environment.

Conserving natural resources

Recycling is an important part of looking after the Earth's natural resources to make sure they are not wasted and do not run out. Natural resources are raw materials taken from the Earth and used to make products. The main raw materials used in glass making are:

- ↻ sand, found in large deposits all over the world
- ↻ lime, made from crushed limestone found in many countries
- ↻ soda ash, made from a mineral called trona which is found in several places including Africa, China, Turkey, and the United States.

When glass is recycled, natural resources remain in the ground and the environment is left undisturbed.

The raw materials used to make glass are cheap and plentiful. However, recycling glass causes less damage to the environment than mining these raw materials.

How limestone mining affects the environment

Limestone is blasted from the ground using explosives, and the shattered rock is dug up and taken away. Explosives scare wildlife away from an area. In some places limestone is dug from deep pits called quarries. No trees and few plants are able to grow again in these deep, empty pits.

Glass is made from sand, soda ash, and lime.

Some old limestone quarries, such as this one in Milburn in New Zealand, are filled with water and turned into lakes.

glass?

How sand mining affects the environment

Sand is mined from beaches, **sand dunes**, and ocean beds. Sand mining removes millions of tons of sand, and, in some places, whole beaches have been removed. When this happens, the ocean tide washes onto the land and carries away plants and soil. The seawater also leaves behind salt, which kills most plants, including large trees. When plants die, birds and other wildlife lose their feeding and breeding grounds.

Turtles are badly affected by sand mining. Turtles return every year to the place where they were born to lay their eggs. Where beaches are mined for sand, turtle populations die out.

When glass is recycled, less sand is mined and fewer plants and wildlife **habitats** are damaged.

Sand mines, such as this one in India, harm plants and wildlife.

"Greener" manufacturing

Recycling is a great way to reduce some of the problems caused when glass is manufactured. Glass products that are not recycled are made in two steps:

1 Melting: The raw materials—sand, soda ash, and lime—are fed into one end of a tank inside a furnace. They are heated until they turn into molten glass.

2 Forming: The molten glass is drawn out the other end of the tank. Some glass is blown into molds to make bottles and jars. Some is drawn out in flat sheets to make windows.

Recycling glass is "greener" than manufacturing new glass products because fewer raw materials are needed and fewer harmful gases are released.

How glass making affects the environment

Glass-making furnaces are heated by burning either petroleum oil or natural gas. These are both **fossil fuels** and **non-renewable** resources. When these fossil fuels burn, they release **carbon dioxide** gas into the atmosphere. Carbon dioxide is one of the gases adding to **global warming** and changing weather patterns worldwide.

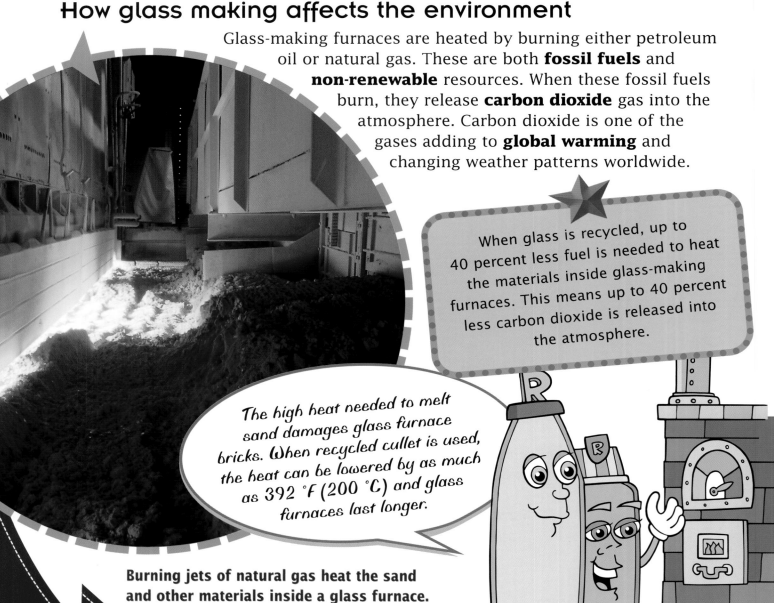

When glass is recycled, up to 40 percent less fuel is needed to heat the materials inside glass-making furnaces. This means up to 40 percent less carbon dioxide is released into the atmosphere.

The high heat needed to melt sand damages glass furnace bricks. When recycled cullet is used, the heat can be lowered by as much as 392 °F (200 °C) and glass furnaces last longer.

Burning jets of natural gas heat the sand and other materials inside a glass furnace.

How melting sand affects the environment

During glass making, fossil fuels must be heated to very high temperatures to melt the sand. Sand melts at temperatures of up to 2,912 °F (1,600 °C). All fossil fuels contain a chemical called nitrogen. When nitrogen burns hotter than 2,552 °F (1,400 °C), it mixes with oxygen in the air and forms **nitrogen oxides**. Nitrogen oxides escaping into the atmosphere create a special type of air pollution called **smog**.

When glass is recycled, less heat is needed to melt the raw materials in the tank inside the glass furnace. This means fewer nitrogen oxides are released and there is less harmful smog.

Smog is a brown-yellow haze that hangs in the air above cities on warm, still days. Smog is made every day when nitrogen oxides escape into the air and are "cooked" by warm sunlight. This makes them combine with smoke fumes from car exhausts, and with floating dust particles from roads and building sites. On days when there is no wind to blow the smog away, it hangs in the air. Smog clouds can cause sore eyes and serious breathing problems.

Glass-making factories add to the smog above industrial cities on warm, still days.

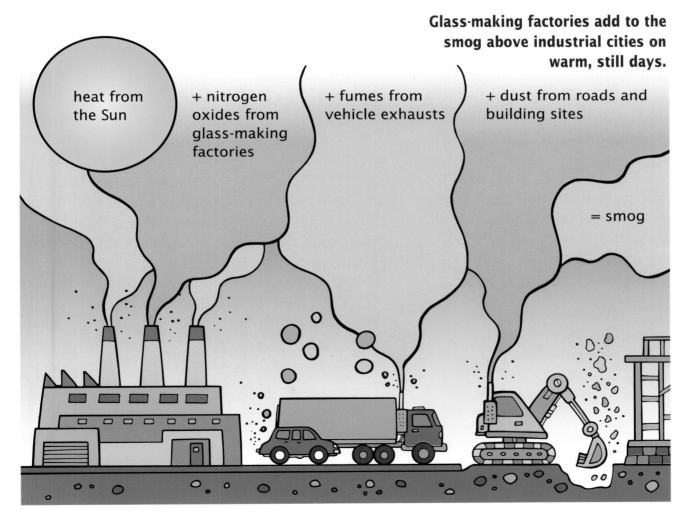

heat from the Sun

+ nitrogen oxides from glass-making factories

+ fumes from vehicle exhausts

+ dust from roads and building sites

= smog

Reducing waste

Billions of tons of glass are thrown away every year, creating troublesome waste. When glass is recycled instead of being thrown away, the amount of waste is reduced and some problems with waste are solved.

Glass in landfills

Landfills are large holes dug in the ground in which waste materials are buried. Glass makes up nine percent of the total volume, or amount of space, of all household waste buried in landfills. Scientists believe it will take one million years for glass to **decompose**, or break down, naturally and return to the soil.

Countries around the world are trying to stop garbage from going to landfills because land is too valuable to use as garbage dumps. Land is needed for farms, towns, factories, and schools. Some countries, such as Japan and Switzerland, have no land left to use as landfills.

When glass is recycled instead of being sent to a landfill, more land is left free for other uses.

Fresh Kills Landfill on Staten Island, New York, is the largest landfill and the largest built object in the world.

If all waste glass in the U.S. and the United Kingdom was recycled, 513 landfills could be closed!

U.S.	= 2,300 landfills
United Kingdom	= 3,400 landfills
Total	= 5,700 landfills

Glass makes up 9% of household waste in landfills

9% of 5,700 = 513 landfills

Glass litter

Some people get rid of their glass waste by throwing it away as litter. Glass litter carelessly thrown away on roadsides, in parks, and dumped in the environment can cause special problems. Glass is easily broken, and every year many people and animals are hurt by stepping or falling on broken glass. Its sharp edges can cause serious cuts and bleeding. Glass can also start fires. Glass can bend rays of sunlight and shine them onto a single point, which produces enough heat to make dry leaves and grass burst into flame.

In hot, wet, tropical climates, discarded glass bottles and jars quickly fill with water and become breeding grounds for mosquitoes. Tropical mosquitoes carry dangerous diseases that kill thousands of people every year. Glass bottles dropped on the ground are also dangerous for small creatures that crawl inside and starve when they cannot get out.

When glass is recycled rather than being thrown away as litter, it is less likely to cause fires or injure people and animals.

A fire that swept through a wildlife reserve in Kenya, Africa, in 1998 is believed to have been started by broken glass. The fire killed many animals, including lions and baboons.

For and against

Question:
Can the Earth sustain its growing population?

Answer:
Yes, if people act now to preserve the environment and manage the Earth's resources better.

Question:
Can this be achieved just by recycling?

"YES" The "yes" case for recycling

✓ Recycling glass reduces the need to mine sand and limestone. This means less harm is done to the environment.

✓ Making glass products from recycled cullet uses up to 40 percent less energy than making glass from raw materials. This reduces air pollution caused by burning fossil fuels, and leaves those fuels in the ground for people in the future to use.

✓ When glass is recycled, less landfill space is needed.

✓ Recycling glass causes less damage to glass furnaces than using raw materials, so furnaces last longer.

✓ Recycling glass reduces the risk of accidental cuts and fires that may harm people and wildlife.

Shelburne Bay in Australia has pure white sand. Pure white sand is the best sand for glass making. The Wuthathi people, Shelburne Bay's traditional owners, have been successful in their fight to protect the land from sand mining.

recycling

Question:
Do most people agree that recycling is a good idea?

Answer:
Yes.

Question:
Will recycling fix all the problems caused by glass manufacturing and glass waste?

"NO" The "no" case against recycling

✗ Glass containers are heavy and trucks use up a lot of valuable fossil fuels collecting glass for recycling. Fossil fuels are expensive and scarce, whereas the raw materials for glass are cheap and plentiful.

✗ Glass collected for recycling is easily **contaminated**. A small amount of aluminum or pottery in a batch of molten glass will ruin the whole batch. Metal lids and stones can damage expensive glass-making furnaces.

Pottery contamination in recycled glass causes weak spots that make glass shatter easily.

✗ Bottle banks cannot always be placed where they are most needed. Glass falling on glass in bottle banks is noisy, and broken glass left lying around bottle banks is dangerous. Most people do not want them in their area.

✗ Some people will use and waste even more glass because glass is being recycled. They may believe that recycling is solving all the problems of mining, manufacturing, and waste disposal, but it is not.

Reduce, reuse,

Recycling is a great idea, but it is just one answer to the problems of how to conserve resources, reduce manufacturing pollution and waste, and protect the environment. There are other things we can do that are even better than recycling. We can reduce, reuse, and rethink what we use.

Reduce

The best and quickest way to reduce glass waste is to use less glass! Reducing is easy. Bottles and jars are the only glass products recycled from household waste. All other glass products, such as saucepans and ornaments, contain metals that contaminate glass cullet. Most of these products end up going to landfills. The best way to reduce glass waste is to buy the same sorts of products made from other materials.

Another way to reduce glass use is to buy long-life lightbulbs. They are made from the same amount of glass, but last up to five times longer than ordinary lightbulbs.

Glass product alternatives

Non-recyclable glass products	The same products made from other materials
glass saucepans	metal saucepans
glass cooktops	metal cooktops
glass cups and plates	china cups and plates
glass coffee plungers	china coffee pots
colored glass ornaments	wooden or metal ornaments
glass doors	wooden doors

rethink

Reuse

A lot of glass products can be used again and again. Some of the ways glass products can be reused are:

- glass jars and bottles can be used to store other things
- in areas where glass bottles are refilled, they can be returned to stores
- unwanted glass items, such as tableware, can be given to charity shops
- unwanted mirrors, windows, and glass doors can be given away or sold.

Refilling glass containers would be easier if they were not made in so many different sizes and shapes.

Rethink

Everyone can come up with new ideas. Some ideas for changing the way we use glass products and materials are:

- more food and drink products could be sold in refillable containers if producers agreed to use bottles and jars of the same sizes and shapes, rather than many different sizes and shapes
- all glass containers could be made of clear glass and coated with a green or brown colored film that melted away during reprocessing. This would end the need for sorting glass containers into pure streams and make glass recycling easier and cheaper.

Wine bottles are usually green and beer bottles are usually brown because the dark color stops sunlight from reaching the drink and changing the flavor.

What governments

Governments around the world are finding ways to encourage people to become more involved in reusing glass, and are rethinking the way glass is collected for recycling.

Passing laws

Prince Edward Island, Canada, attracts thousands of tourists each year. Unfortunately, these tourists were littering the island's roads, fields, and beaches with thousands of disposable bottles and cans. The island has very little landfill space, and no recycling factories for plastics, metals, or glass. Getting rid of this litter was a big problem. However, the island did have a drink manufacturer with equipment for washing and refilling glass bottles.

The government of Prince Edward Island decided to pass a law banning all types of drink containers except refillable glass. A deposit tax, placed on refillable glass bottles, encourages people to return the bottles to stores and get the deposit money back. With this law, Prince Edward Island has achieved the highest glass recovery rate in the world, almost 99 percent.

GOVERNMENT APPROVED

OFFICIAL GLASS POLICY

A law banning all non-refillable drink containers has cleaned up litter from the beautiful beaches of Prince Edward Island, Canada.

are doing

Collecting glass

Glass is one of the most difficult materials to collect for recycling. The problems with collecting glass are:

- glass is bulky and takes up a lot of space
- bottle banks fill up quickly and glass is often left on the ground
- glass falling on glass is very noisy and people do not want to live near bottle banks.

The local government in the old Dutch city of Dordrecht came up with a way of collecting glass that overcomes these problems. They built bottle banks underneath the sidewalks. Bottles and jars are deposited into the banks through slim metal tubes that stand just 3.3 feet (1 m) high. There are three tubes, one for each glass color: clear, green, and brown. Because the banks are underground, the sound of glass falling on glass is not so loud. Each container can hold up to five times more glass than normal above-ground bins. An automatic weighing system beneath the bins tells collectors when the bins are ready to be emptied, so they never overflow.

The city of Dordrecht, in the Netherlands, uses underground bottle banks.

GOVERNMENT APPROVED

The automatic weighing system tells collectors when the bins are ready to be emptied.

What industries are

Industries are using recycled glass in interesting ways. They are also finding ways to collect more glass for recycling, to reuse glass, and to rethink their glass use.

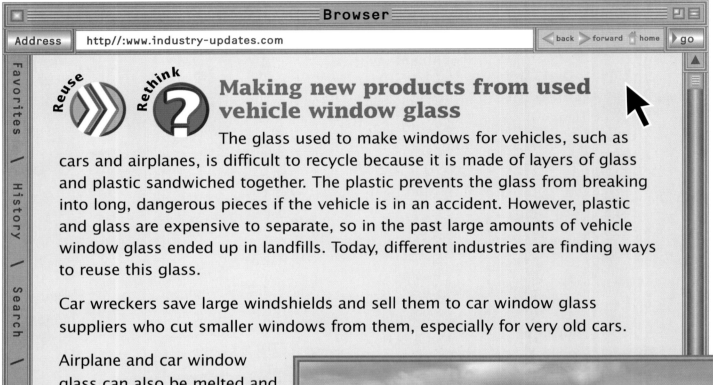

Browser

Address http//:www.industry-updates.com   back   forward   home   go

Favorites | History | Search | Scrapbook | Page Holder

Reuse   Rethink ?

Making new products from used vehicle window glass

The glass used to make windows for vehicles, such as cars and airplanes, is difficult to recycle because it is made of layers of glass and plastic sandwiched together. The plastic prevents the glass from breaking into long, dangerous pieces if the vehicle is in an accident. However, plastic and glass are expensive to separate, so in the past large amounts of vehicle window glass ended up in landfills. Today, different industries are finding ways to reuse this glass.

Car wreckers save large windshields and sell them to car window glass suppliers who cut smaller windows from them, especially for very old cars.

Airplane and car window glass can also be melted and mixed with colored cement to make hard-wearing work surfaces, such as kitchen benchtops. Used vehicle window glass is also melted and mixed with clay and a coloring agent, then hardened to make different colored wall and floor tiles.

Some old cars have small windows. Replacement windows can be cut from used, modern car windshields.

doing

Favorites \ History \ Search \ Scrapbook \ Page Holder

Recycle

Better glass collection

ACI Glass manufacturers in Australia wanted to use recycled glass, because making glass from recycled cullet saves energy. However, ACI had to throw away many loads of used glass because the glass was contaminated with metal and plastic scraps.

Then ACI tried a new idea. They got garbage collectors in the city of Sydney to contact thousands of clubs, hotels, and restaurants that sell large quantities of drinks in glass bottles. ACI gave each business one or more 16-gallon (60-l) recycling crates from Visy Recycling. The crates were placed near bars, kitchens, or places where people could deposit bottles easily after use. ACI also printed posters for clubs and hotels, telling customers about the recycling program.

ACI gave local businesses 16-gallon (60-l) Visy Recycling crates for storing their recyclable glass.

Each business paid their local garbage collector a small fee to empty the 16-gallon (60-l) crates and take the glass to ACI. This fee was less than the cost of taking waste glass to a landfill by truck. ACI was happy to buy the glass from the garbage collectors, because it contained very few materials that would contaminate the glass. ACI has now set up the same program in other areas.

What communities

People working together in communities are finding new and interesting ways to recycle, reuse, and rethink glass use.

Sunday October 25

Your local newspaper

THE DAILY HERALD

Morning edition

Boulton Elementary School won the Derby glass recycling competition in 2002. The school received a check from Jenny Jar, a glass recycling mascot.

Rethink ❓ New ideas

The St. Vincent de Paul charity organization in Oregon came up with an idea to keep tons of waste glass out of landfills. They set up the Aurora Glass **Foundry** and started using waste glass to make beautiful glass art objects. The glass art is sold in shops and over the Internet. The money raised is used to help homeless and jobless people.

Recycle ♻ Recycling more

The city of Derby in England, United Kingdom, runs a school glass recycling competition every year. Students at each school get families and friends to deposit all their used glass in the bottle bank closest to their school. The glass collected from each bottle bank is weighed, and a record is kept of every load. The 2002 competition was won by Boulton Elementary School. First prize was £1,000 (about $1,750). During the 10 weeks of the 2002 competition, an extra 55,000 bottles were collected for recycling.

Workers at the St. Vincent de Paul's Aurora Glass Foundry make beautiful glass objects from waste glass.

are doing

Reuse

Building with glass bottles

La Casita Verde (The Little Green House) is an **ecological center** on the island of Ibiza, off the coast of Spain. It is a community of people from all over the world who got together to show others how to live in harmony with nature. They take only what they need from their environment, and create no unnecessary waste. At La Casita Verde, all materials are recycled, even building materials. One special dwelling was built entirely from waste materials found around the island, including hundreds of glass bottles.

The bottle house at La Casita Verde, Spain, is made from waste materials including hundreds of glass bottles.

The bottles were collected over time from local bars and restaurants. The walls of the dwelling were made by laying glass bottles on their sides, like bricks, and cementing them together with a mixture of red earth and straw. Bottles are a good building material. They are strong, and the air inside them helps to keep buildings warm in winter and cool in summer. The door and windows of the bottle house were rescued from local dumpsters, and the roof is an 11-foot (3.5-m) metal dish once used for receiving satellite signals.

The glass bottles keep the bottle house warm in winter and cool in summer.

What individuals

Individuals are coming up with new ideas and inspiring others about recycling glass.

Individuals making your planet a better place.

Green Fingers Newsletter

Rethink?

Weaving glass art

Richard Lloyd became interested in glass making while serving as a peacekeeper with the New Zealand Army in Lebanon. There he watched glass artists fire glass in small furnaces, called kilns, and create beautiful glassware by hand. When Lloyd came home, he left the army and built his own glass kiln, using pieces of old exercise equipment. Lloyd believed that any piece of glass could be made into something else and should not be wasted.

For a year, Lloyd collected glass, crushed it by hand, and experimented with firing and shaping it. Other glass artists told him it was impossible to weave glass. Lloyd took up the challenge and 18 months later found a way to do it. In 1994, Lloyd set up the Waitaha Glass Foundry. There workers use recycled glass to make glass art objects and glass floor tiles.

As part of his commitment to recycling, Lloyd also runs the Recovered Materials Foundation (RMF) in Christchurch. The RMF helps people start new businesses reusing and recycling waste materials.

Richard Lloyd makes beautiful woven glass creations.

are doing

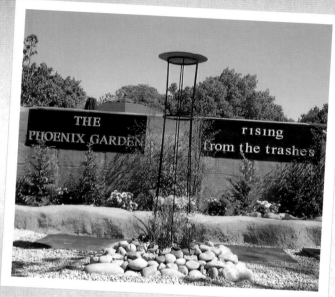

The Garden of Recovery was created from recycled glass by Maxine Childs and Gina Payne in Christchurch, New Zealand.

Recycle
Making a glass garden landscape

New Zealand garden designers, Maxine Childs and Gina Payne, took on a special project to remind the people of Christchurch about recycling glass. Using products made from waste glass, they created a unique garden landscape in one of the city's parks. The garden wall was made from straw bales covered with textured-glass coating. Part of the walkway was a glass carpet showing a picture of a phoenix bird. A phoenix is a make-believe bird that was said to burn up in order to be born again. Bottles were used as candle lamps and a recycled glass sculpture stood at the center. Childs and Payne called their garden the Garden of Recovery.

Recycle
Recycling glass bottles

Englishman John Barrett gave up work in atomic energy research to become a glass artist. Barrett invented a process for turning waste glass bottles into flat pieces of colored glass that can be used to make beautiful stained glass windows. In 1997, Barrett and six friends set up the Recycled Bottle Glass Center in Plymouth, England, United Kingdom. Barrett visits schools and helps students create stained glass windows from recycled glass.

John Barrett helped students at Stoke Dameral Community College in the United Kingdom to design this stained glass window made from recycled glass.

What you can do

You can do all sorts of activities to help recycle, reduce, and reuse glass. You can also get others interested and come up with ideas to stop glass from harming the environment. Make a weekly "Glass 3-R scorecard" for yourself or your class.

What to do:

1 Draw up a scorecard with headings like the one shown below.
2 Write down each time you or your class do something to recycle, reduce, or reuse glass.
3 Reward yourself or your class with a green star for each activity that you do.

Glass 3-R scorecard

Recycle	Reduce	Reuse	Get others interested	Other things
Washed out glass bottles for recycling.	Mom and I made tomato ketchup instead of buying bottled ketchup.	Put our tomato ketchup in old (clean) ketchup bottles.	Talked to Mrs. Lilly about recycling her glass bottles instead of trashing them.	Mom and I picked up two bottles that were littering the park.
Dad and I took Mrs. Lilly's bottles to the bottle bank on the way to the library.	Bought olive oil in a can instead of glass.	Filled a glass jar with shells as a bathroom ornament.	Asked Mom to find out if we can buy milk in refillable bottles.	E-mailed the council and asked them to please empty the bottle bank. It's overflowing!
	Got long-life lightbulbs that use less power and save glass.	Reused my glass fish tank as a terrarium garden.	Made a glass recycling poster for the local liquor store.	

Get others interested

You can make a poster or leaflets to show others how to recycle glass. Most people want to recycle their waste glass but are not sure how.

GLASS RECYCLING

> A bold heading will catch people's attention.

WHAT CAN BE RECYCLED?

YES
- ✓ glass food jars
- ✓ glass drink bottles

> List the types of glass that can be recycled.

NO
- ✗ window glass or mirrors
- ✗ cookware or tableware
- ✗ pottery plates, bowls, and mugs
- ✗ lightbulbs
- ✗ TV picture tubes

> List the types of glass that cannot be recycled.

> A small amount of any of these materials can ruin a whole batch of recycled glass.

HOW TO RECYCLE:

1. Rinse bottles and jars in used dishwashing water.

> This avoids attracting ants, cockroaches, and bees, and avoids bad smells.

2. Remove metal and plastic lids.

> You do not have to remove labels. The high temperature of glass processing burns them away.

3. Clear, green, and brown glass only.

4. No broken glass, please.

> Broken glass can harm other recyclers, collectors, or process workers.

 Thank you for recycling.

> Add interest to your leaflets with pictures or computer clip art images.

Decomposition timeline

This timeline shows how long it takes for products and materials to break down and return to the soil when left exposed to air and sunlight.

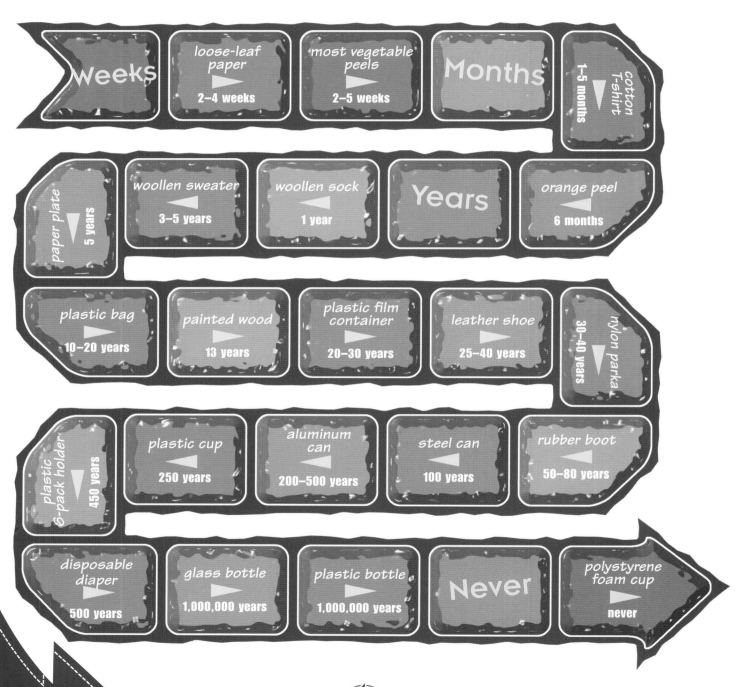

Weeks

loose-leaf paper
2–4 weeks

most vegetable peels
2–5 weeks

Months

cotton T-shirt
1–5 months

paper plate
5 years

woollen sweater
3–5 years

woollen sock
1 year

Years

orange peel
6 months

plastic bag
10–20 years

painted wood
13 years

plastic film container
20–30 years

leather shoe
25–40 years

nylon parka
30–40 years

plastic 6-pack holder
450 years

plastic cup
250 years

aluminum can
200–500 years

steel can
100 years

rubber boot
50–80 years

disposable diaper
500 years

glass bottle
1,000,000 years

plastic bottle
1,000,000 years

Never

polystyrene foam cup
never

Glossary

asphalt a mix of tar and gravel used for making roads and other hard surfaces

carbon dioxide a gas breathed out by people and animals and taken in by trees, and also released by burning fossil fuels

contaminated ruined by harmful material; recycled glass can be contaminated by aluminum or pottery

cullet crushed glass

decompose to break down into simple substances through the activity of tiny living organisms called bacteria

developed countries countries where most people have good living conditions and use a lot of manufactured products

ecological center a place where people learn about helping the environment

fiberglass a tough blend of glass fibers and plastic

fossil fuels fuels, such as petroleum, coal, and natural gas, which formed from the remains of ancient plants and animals

foundry a factory where materials such as glass and metal are melted and cast in molds

furnace a very hot oven used to melt materials, such as glass, or to heat the raw materials used to make glass

glazing a thin layer of glass put over pottery to make it waterproof

global warming warming of the Earth's atmosphere due to the build-up of heat-holding gases

habitats areas where particular plants and animals live and breed

landfills large holes in the ground in which waste materials are buried

molten melted into a liquid by heat

natural resources materials taken from the Earth and used to make products, such as sand used to make glass

nitrogen oxides gases released by very hot fossil fuels, which create smog

non-renewable cannot be made or grown again

pollution dirty or harmful waste material that damages air, water, or land

pure streams lots of glass items of the same color

raw materials materials that have not been processed or treated before, such as sand mined from beaches, sand dunes, and ocean beds

reprocessing using glass again to make new glass products

sand dunes large hills of sand moved and shaped by wind

smog a brown-yellow haze that forms over industrial cities (**sm**oke and f**og**)

Index